YOUR KNOWLEDGE HAS VALUE

- We will publish your bachelor's and master's thesis, essays and papers

- Your own eBook and book - sold worldwide in all relevant shops

- Earn money with each sale

Upload your text at www.GRIN.com
and publish for free

Mohamed Hajji

Aus der Reihe: e-fellows.net stipendiaten-wissen

e-fellows.net (Hrsg.)

Band 1453

A Review on the Economic Calculation Debate

Did modern theorists really misunderstand Hayek's insights?

GRIN Publishing

Bibliographic information published by the German National Library:

The German National Library lists this publication in the National Bibliography; detailed bibliographic data are available on the Internet at http://dnb.dnb.de .

Imprint:

Copyright © 2015 GRIN Verlag GmbH
Print and binding: Books on Demand GmbH, Norderstedt Germany
ISBN: 978-3-656-97844-2

This book at GRIN:

http://www.grin.com/en/e-book/300191/a-review-on-the-economic-calculation-debate

GRIN - Your knowledge has value

Since its foundation in 1998, GRIN has specialized in publishing academic texts by students, college teachers and other academics as e-book and printed book. The website www.grin.com is an ideal platform for presenting term papers, final papers, scientific essays, dissertations and specialist books.

Visit us on the internet:

http://www.grin.com/

http://www.facebook.com/grincom

http://www.twitter.com/grin_com

Department of Economics
Witten/Herdecke University

A REVIEW ON THE ECONOMIC CALCULATION DEBATE
Did modern theorists really misunderstand Hayek´s insights?

31-March-2015

Author: Mohamed Hajji
Course: *History of Economic Thought II*
The Utopia of Control: Market Socialism in the History of Economics

I.   Introduction

Friedrich August von Hayek is well known as a rigor criticizer of market socialism. His contribution to the socialist calculation debates was difficult, to interpret for modern information theorists and mechanism design theorists. In this regard, many theorists have misunderstood Hayek´s contribution to the socialist calculation debate until today. Therefore, the question still arises: Did modern theorists really misunderstand Hayek´s insight?

The answer to this question can be found by understanding Professor Caldwell's arguments in his paper just mentioned above and various studies referring to the discourse of the calculation debates.

In the paper *Hayek and Socialism*, Professor Caldwell analyzes Hayek´s participation in the socialist calculation debate from the 1930s and 1940s. Furthermore, he reviews the new debate on market socialism. The particularity was that he considers the intellectual environment in which Hayek's thought was evolved.

Hayek was involved in a variety of discussions with advocates for the market socialism such as Lange and Lerner. One of his essential contributions to the calculation debates was published in *Collectivist Economic Planning* and includes a series of essays like *Individualism and Economic Order, Economic and Knowledge, The Use of Knowledge in Society* and *The Meaning of Competition*. In general, they contain Hayek´s explanation for the failure of the market socialism and further throw light on difficulties caused by state interventionism that still exist today.

In recent debates about the calculation problems the economics of information introduce themselves by Bardhan, Roemer (1995), J. Stiglitz (1994) and others who claim that the main reason for the break-up of the communistic regime due to information asymmetries and related incentive compatibility. In contrast, Hayek did not contribute significantly to economics of information, though he never tried to change science of economics. His main aim was to improve social conditions of the society in his day.

The sections (II) will demonstrate that Hayek's insight related to socialist calculation debates was understood by the majority of information theorists as it applies the progress in this field nowadays, which Hayek sought to show. Section (III) will examine Professor Caldwell's argumentation. The final section will conclude the implications drawn from the answers to the question of the essay.

II. A question of interpretation?

Hayek's work on the "dispersion of knowledge" is widely known and had played an important role in developing Hayek's ideas and implications on the calculation debate. He claims in his article *Economic and Knowledge (1937)* that the central planners are facing the knowledge problem with respect to plan production and price goods. He examines that information cannot be easily collected or conveyed, because it is dispersed and possessed by individuals. Moreover, individuals do not recognize sometimes the value of the knowledge that they own. They possess localized knowledge in other words *"knowledge of the particular circumstances of time and place"*. (Hayek 1945, p. 80) At the same time, there is tacit knowledge that is difficult to convey to central planners or other individuals. Furthermore, individuals may have no incentives to share the knowledge. As a result, Hayek´s emphasizes the point to utilize the dispersed knowledge in the market by acquiring data through price signals. In this context, Professor Caldwell examines that modern information theorists did not have a profound understanding about tacit and localized knowledge, however, they were able to understand the domain that prices convey information and that knowledge is dispersed. For instance, Sanford Grossman, a modern information theorist has acknowledged that market prices convey information. He continued working on this idea from Hayek together with Joseph Stiglitz, by analyzing situations in which individuals infer information from market prices. In addition, Hayek´s idea was incorporated into the modern mainstream economics after a while. [1] In particular, Leonid Huriwicz, a pioneer of the "mechanism design" theory has credited and later advanced Hayek´s insight given in the paper *"The Use of Knowledge in Society" (1945)*. This indicates that some information theorists and methodology theorists indeed understood Hayek. Even though, they did not grasp a deeper understanding of Hayek´s insights. We must consider that otherwise his two key papers mentioned above would be left out in the science of economics. Subsequently, Hayek was not totally misunderstood. This might be also a reason why today modern theorists are more familiar with the "dispersion of knowledge" arguments of Hayek.

Second, Professor Caldwell claims that the methodology design theorists and mainstream economists misunderstood Hayek because they misinterpret his book *The Road of Serfdom (1945)* as a prediction instead of a warning. He supports his claim by

---

[1] Steven Horwitz, *Microfoundation and Macroecnomics – An Austrian Perspective*, 2000, p. 31

determining that methodology theorist tried to investigate an existence of historical patterns or trends. Whereas, Hayek does not acknowledge a consistence of repeating stages in the human history, Professor Caldwell stated. Likewise, when Hayek wrote the book he had in mind Great Britain, as in fact, no historical events took place over in this country. Taking this into consideration it might be the case, that methodology theorists misread Hayek´s warning rather than misunderstood him. Because of that, they indeed understand his main conclusion of the book that planning must necessarily and inevitably lead to authoritarianism. Clearly, we can reject and weight Professor Caldwell's argument as weak in this respect and conclude, that no real misconception exist at this point. Accordingly, methodology design theorists did not misunderstood Hayek, in this respect.

Third, we should draw to the fact that Hayek similar to the modern information theorists understood that the theoretical tools were insufficient for understanding the limitations of socialism, as Professor Caldwell argued. That means, in this case no misconstrue did exist between Hayek and modern information theorists. The only difference was that Hayek identified the impractical treatment of knowledge as a main cause. For Hayek, the neoclassical theory was useless and not really helpful. He did not agree on perfect competition, the idea of "given" knowledge and homo oeconomicus. He characterized the market as a dynamic market process where rivalry among participants ensures that knowledge is generated and discovered not as mainstream economist believe in the idea of "search". Although, modern theorists had different interpretations on the causes of the limitation of socialism they did evidently share with Hayek the same view about the theoretical restrictiveness. As result, once again Hayek was understood. This might be also a hint why most of theoretical models progressed based on the socialist calculation debate in the economics, for example, they contain the sophisticated understanding of agency problems.

Professor Caldwell just offers an image of the world in his paper. As it is clear, that he has a given sympathy for Hayek´s work. As you can see in following paragraph, for instance: *"It nonetheless remains an impressive attempt to construct an integrated system of social philosophy, ethics, jurisprudence and intellectual history. And it is hard to deny Hayek´s foundational contention that a liberal order allows individual knowledge is better used than does socialism."* *(Caldwell 1997, p. 1871)* It can be easily seen that Professor Caldwell's view might be incomplete, because he influences the reader by just choosing those scholars who did misinterpret Hayek´s work in the past. Besides, his perspective is very broad on Hayek´s work. Therefore, he did not just cover Hayek´s work related on economy theory, but also from several other disciplines. That is why he stresses the question if modern theorists misunderstood Hayek. The claim might be easier to argue if he would exclude Hayek´s work based on other fields and just discuss his work based on an economical foundation. Because of the fact, that many scholars did not explore resolutions for the calculation debate outside of the science of economics. Hence, we are confronted with a one-sided perspective.

However, scholars criticize hat Hayek was not really precise in his explanations about his perspective on economics. That is the reason why many opponents and others criticized him in order to better understood his position and arguments. For instance, in Hayek´s reviews to Boris Brutzkus, Henry D. Dickson (1993) and Marxist Dopp (1993) according to the "mathematical solution". Hayek wanted to shift the debate more into the real word as opposed to the static world of perfect competition. Hayek had a broad view on arguments against socialism. He argued that there is not only the problem to gather all the necessary information in order to calculate prices and quantities, but also perfect competition would arise other problems under socialism. Hence, he continued with underlying the concern that central planners would have to take over the role-played by thousands of entrepreneurs in a market system. At this point, Professor Caldwell revealed, Hayek did not really specify the nature of the problem in order to have a better understanding of his insights. Consequently, many modern theorists had a hard time to understand fully Hayek´s position. The reason for that might be that he was seeking for arguments outside of the science of economics.

III. Reasons for misconceptions

Caldwell wrote, *"Now especially in mid-century, most of Hayek's readers would have thought it quaint to consider the market system as a paradigmatic example of a self-organizing system. For them it was more like a machine that had broken down, something that required radical repair, if not outright replacement."* (Caldwell 1997, p. 1871) Socialist thought that central planning is a rational order. Hayek attacked that viewpoint harshly. This is a fallacy according to Hayek who asserts that the economy is a necessary spontaneous order and it cannot be intentionally designed. He criticized scholars and policy makers who thought that without a social system there would be an irrational and by accident designed system existing. To that extent, he opens up a given rise of misconceptions of Hayek´s work, which has early, began. The reason for this might be unknown ignorance.

In the first place, Hayek's contribution against socialism should not be linked to historical background, stated Professor Caldwell right in the beginning of his paper. Indeed, modern information theorists should take Hayek's arguments into a less historical context and assess Hayek's set of claims against socialism as an independent set of claims against socialism as Professor Caldwell examined in his paper.

In this regard, Professor Caldwell does exactly the opposite on page 1880, where he argues with a historical treatment in order to support his statement on why Hayek did not pursue to follow the incentive question. *"Modern theorists might concede the historical point." (Caldwell 1997, p. 1880)* He exposed that the historical context has not shed much light on the incentive question. However, it is contradictory of what he early argued in his paper. Taking both paragraphs into consideration, indeed the historical context may help to understand Hayek's insights or the way Hayek went in the past. Besides the fact, that at this time Oskar Lange did also not carry on the incentive problems, for him the question was related to the subject of sociology. At latest, Professor Caldwell argues that *[...] those who would try to read history backwards, [...] would assess Hayek's contribution solely in terms of whether and how he anticipated the later literature on the economics of information, will perforce misunderstand his arguments against socialism. (Caldwell 1997, p.1857)* To put it in a nutshell, he examines the historical treatment as a reason for why modern economist did misunderstand Hayek's insights.

Next, Hayek's contribution in the new debate on market socialism was still misunderstood, Professor Caldwell examines that modern theorists did not really pose and highlighted Hayek´s problems that he faced to answer, because of the fact that they targeted different questions in their research program. Hayek concentrated on areas that are not emphasized by modern information theorists. While, mainstream and methodology theorists were focusing on how markets "convey" information. He argues that Hayek had a much broader investigation by considering the creation, discovery, and conservation of knowledge. Even though they had a different image of the market process itself. The notion of "discovery" was distinctive to the idea of "search" that they had in mind. Likewise, Professor Caldwell observes that Lange, the soviet planer and modern information theorist misunderstands a crucial point in the Austrian analysis. The fact that there is no guarantee of coordination, but indeed a system in which prices determined in competitive markets are free to adjust to reflect relative scarcities is one in which the coordination of agents plans is least likely to be hindered. (Caldwell 1997, p.1883) Mainstream theorists note the importance of competition within a market system but they missed the relevance of discovery in the market process by errors, new products and processes, of knowledge itself. In that, they defined errors as disequilibrium phenomena.

The discussion provides an order of causes why Hayek was actually misunderstood. Hayek´s thinking was very unfamiliar to them. That is why modernist were not able to reveal explicitly their theories to Hayek´s ideas.

Furthermore, Professor Caldwell examines regarding the incentive question between information theorists, mainstream economics, Hayek and the Austrians that Hayek was not completely familiar with the subject. He pointed out, that Hayek did not want to be drawn into the incentive problems which socialism have faced. The reason for that he examined was the complexity; subtlety and the historical context have not shed much light on that issue. (Caldwell 1997, p. 1880) As a consequence, modern information theorists claim that Hayek and the Austrians significantly have misled the incentive question, because they failed to provide a systematic analysis of the problem arising from information asymmetric. To someone who held this position above, Professor Caldwell contended that Hayek evidently outlines incentive issues in the final of *Collectivist Economic Planning (1935)*. The "Russian experiment" showed that *"it is difficult that people follow out the plan loyally." (Hayek 1935; p.206)* He also added that Peter Boettke (1995) has interpreted in some parts of *The Road to Serfdom* that Hayek noted how institutions affect the incentive agents face in order to support his thesis. Finally, Professor Caldwell stated that the modern theorist rather misunderstood Hayek than Hayek and the Austrians ignored the incentive question.

As mentioned earlier, for Hayek knowledge is dispersed as later mechanism design theorists picked up on. (Caldwell 1997, p.1882) But nevertheless, they miss the point that no designed mechanism can elicit tacit knowledge. They treat knowledge as little packages that can be collected. But in fact, tacit knowledge is hard to communicate. Not because it symbolizes any specific knowledge or expertise, but rather it is defined by the day-to-day experience over time between market participants. Moreover, tacit knowledge is crucial for entrepreneurs because it influences their decision-making process and ultimately, it reflects the prices and options in a free market system. Here, Professor Caldwell does not really specify why mechanism design theorists were not able to understand the meaning of tacit knowledge and how it is convertible. However, he emphasized the following statement: *"But it should also be clear that when he used the term "knowledge," he was referring to something, that is different in kind from the con-cept of "information" as it is used by current theorists. " (Caldwell, 1997, p.1882)* Don

Lavoie (1985) argued that one must read [...] Hayek's arguments as two sides of the same coin, and Boettke followed him in this regard [...]. [2] It may therefore be concluded, that another reason why Hayek was misunderstood is that the current theorists have mislead to define his terminologies accurately.

One final point, Professor Caldwell argues that Hayek was misunderstood among the modern theorists because of Hayek's work *The Sensory Order* which most of the economic theorists never have read. In fact, the book does not even deal with socialism. Indeed, it is about the link between mind, knowledge and human actions from a psychological perspective. Hayek was looking beyond the science of economics for a new methodology in order to find answers for his questions. In addition, other scholars say that he was not satisfied with the developments of psychology. Unfortunately, economists do not nearly follow the theoretical framework of cultural evolution. Therefore, an important but also controversial piece of Hayek's work was not taken into consideration by modern theorist in order to understand fully his arguments against equilibrium theory and standard theory.

The book does not deal even peripherally with socialism. But properly understood it provides a key for comprehending the nature and extent of Hayek's divergence from mainstream economics in the postwar period, and so may help to explain why modern information theorists writing about market socialism have had such a hard time understanding him (Caldwell 1997, p. 1873).

Consequently, to appreciate Hayek's work it is essential to know that he did not only

---

[2] Boettke, P. (ed.) (2000) *Socialism and the Market Economy: The Socialist Calculation Debate Reconsidered,* 9 vols., London: Routledge.

contribute to the social science and political economics, but also to the field of psychology. His interest in psychology helps to understand how Hayek has developed his thinking. In the latter case, modern theorist did not recognize this significance. As a result, it was difficult for modern information theorists to get behind Hayek´s insight.

IV. Conclusions

While other scholars have recaptured and discussed Hayek´s contribution to the socialist calculation debates, this essay sought to examine the source of construe or misconstrue of Hayek´s work by weighting Professor Caldwell's arguments in his paper *Hayek and Socialism* from 1997.

Fact is Hayek´s favor against the socialism, but he did not clearly point out his arguments. One of the reasons might be sought in his papers, which are either conventional, complex or multi-dimensional written. This circumstance strengthens the opinion that modernists face difficulties to get behind his unorthodox thinking. Hayek deals with different topics on complexity theory and evolutionary biology. Furthermore, his experience and broad interest in different sciences have driven him to change his arguments to various subjects. In consequence, economic theorists had a profound problem to understand Hayek´s position. Therefore, it follows many economists developed false claims against Hayek´s economic written work. Finally, there is no doubt of Professor Caldwell hypothesis towards the question: Did modern theorists really misunderstood Hayek's insight? Nevertheless, further research need be done in order to understand the reasons and to underpin why he has been misunderstood by current theorists.

References:

Bardhan, Pranab and Roemer, John (1993). Market Socialism. *New York and Oxford: Oxford University Press.*

Boettke, P. (ed.) (2000). Socialism and the Market Economy: The Socialist Calculation Debate Reconsidered, 9 vols., *London: Routledge.*

Caldwell, Bruce. (1997). Hayek and Socialism. *Journal of Economic Literature,* 35(4): 1856-90.

Caldwell, B. J. (2004). Hayek's Challenge. *Chicago: University of Chicago Press.*

F.A. Hayek (1937). Economics and Knowledge. *Economica4:* 33–54.

F.A. Hayek (1945): The Use of Knowledge in Society. *American Economic Review* 35 (519–30).

Hayek, F.A. (1948) *Individualism and Economic Order.* Chicago: University of Chicago Press.

Smith, Vernon L. (2003). *Constructivist and Ecological Rationality in Economics. American Economic Review.* 93(3): 465-508.

CPSIA information can be obtained
at www.ICGtesting.com
Printed in the USA
LVIC06n0351150518
577227LV00006B/20